Dedicated to my little pirates,
Riley, Hunter, Kason, Henry,
Ursula, and Braedon.

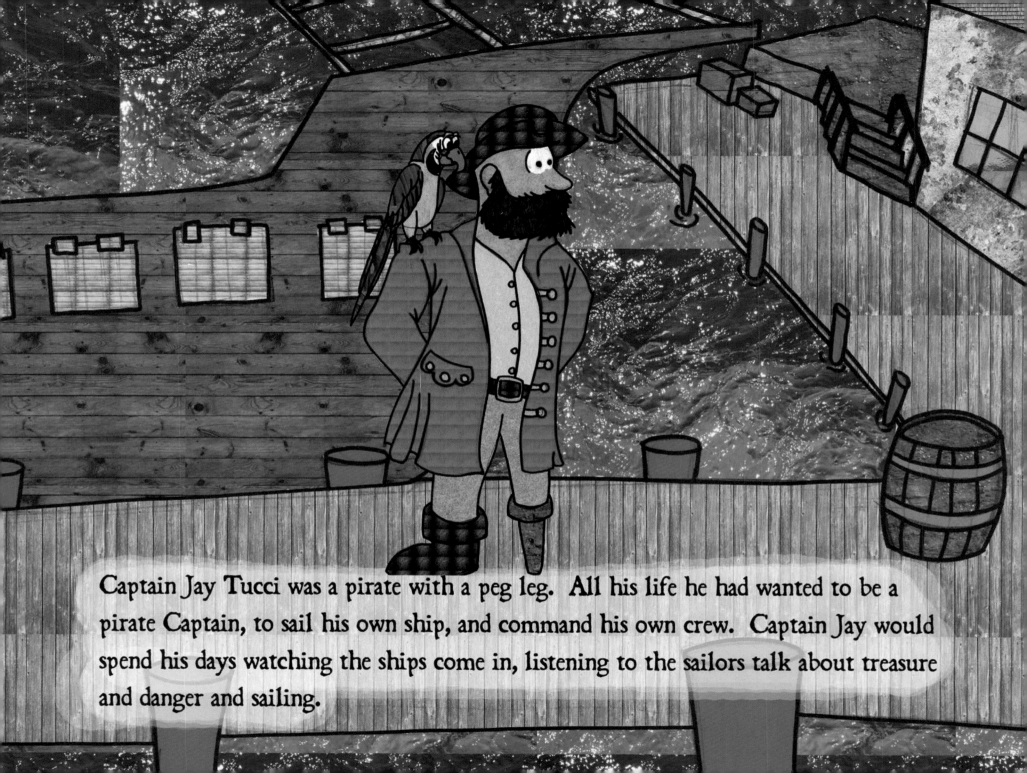

Captain Jay Tucci was a pirate with a peg leg. All his life he had wanted to be a pirate Captain, to sail his own ship, and command his own crew. Captain Jay would spend his days watching the ships come in, listening to the sailors talk about treasure and danger and sailing.

He watched them tie knots, and hoist the sails. He followed them as they bought supplies and counted their treasure. He learned all the best pirate words, like "ARRR" and "Yo Ho Ho", and he studied all the pirate stories about Sea Monsters and ship wrecks.

Captain Jay worked hard helping out on the docks. Every day he did chores and eventually he even saved up enough money to buy his own ship! He named it The Adventure.

Captain Jay was very excited to start his career as a pirate Captain! So, on September 19th, he grabbed his peg, and his trusty friend Tiki, and boarded his ship.

Captain Jay looked around smiling from ear to ear, taking in the wonder that was his ship. "Hoist the sails" He wailed. "Weigh anchor" he exclaimed. "Captain on deck!" He yelled. Nothing happened. Captain Jay looked around, and laughed "Yar har har har, I forgot, I needs me a crew!"

Captain Jay and Tiki set off into town looking for a crew. The other Captains all stared, and pointed, and laughed.

"Look at his peg leg, he can't be a Captain. He can't even walk right!" said one nasty old pirate.

"Yar, he will be the slowest pirate in town har har har" another pirate jeered.

Captain Jay ignored them. His peg leg never stopped him before and it wouldn't stop him now!

All the other Captains turned their backs, set their sails and went off to find treasure, leaving Captain Jay behind

Captain Jay and Tiki went from tavern to tavern and from inn to inn. They searched high, and they searched low. They looked in nooks, and they looked in crannies

After searching for many days, Captain Jay and Tiki stumbled into a dark and deserted part of town. There was a small tavern set way in the back, the roof was rickety, and the door hung on one hinge. They walked into the tavern, noticing the sign, Misfits' Recluse" and set their eyes on the last pirates left in town.

Captain Jay got excited and shouted with glee "AHOY!!! Any of ye scurvy lot wish to join me crew?"

The pirates looked up, saddened, and one stood up and approached Captain Jay. "We can't be pirates, and we can't sail the seas!"

Captain Jay asked "Well why not! Ye look like pirates, ye smell like pirates, and yer even dressed like pirates!"

The man looked back "Can't ye see? We all be different! The other pirate Captains told us all...we can't be pirates, cuz I has only one eye!"

"And I has only one hand" said another.

"And I'm too short!" shouted one more.

"And me nose be too big!" Said the man in the back.

"and that one over there.....he can't hear! Him in the corner, he walks with a stick! Ye see, we all be different, and the other Captains said we can't be pirates like them."

Captain Jay looked around....he saw the big nose, and the one hand. He saw the cane, and the shor man. He saw all these pirates and all the things that made them different, and he smiled! "Well I be Captain Jay, and I has only one leg, so ye know what? I be different too! That doesn't mean we can't be what we want to be! I'll take the lot of ye on me ship and find work for everyone!" The pirates cheered together "YO HO HO! YAR HAR HAR!"

The next day the pirates were all together aboard The Adventure. Some were tending to the sails, others were swabbing the decks. One was checking the crows nest.

Captain Jay was walking around looking at his crew and inspecting their work when the pirate who couldn't hear approached him. The pirate handed Captain Jay a bottle. In the bottle was a letter.

"To anyone still in town, HELP!!!! We pirate captains have been kidnapped. All of arr ships and all of arr crews taken. A giant Kraken has us caught in his arms. We need HELP!"

Captain Jay read the note aloud. When he was done he calmly rolled it up and placed it in his pocket. The crew was staring at him, eyes waiting.

"Well me crew," said Captain Jay "what are we waiting for? We have some pirates to rescue!"

And with a large cheer "HUUZZAAAHHH" the crew got to work. They set sail to find the Kraken, and the pirate prisoners.

It took three days to sail to the Kraken, and when they arrived, the Kraken sat waiting. It saw Captain Jay and his crew, and licked its lips hungrily, excited to have more pirates for his prize. The other Captains and crews looked out, and saw Captain Jay and his crew. "Oh no!" they yelled.

"Captain Jay can't save us, he's only got one leg! And his crew arrr all misfits like him!" Captain Jay gave a wink to the crew, and everyone snapped to work.

The pirate that walked with a stick, wasn't very fast, but he was skilled at making nets. While the ship sailed searching for the Kraken, he spent his time making a large net so the pirates could capture the Kraken.

The pirate with the large nose, smelled the stench of the Kraken, well before they could see it. He shouted to the crew, "Kraken dead ahead!", and the crew prepared themselves for the beast!

The pirate with one eye, who could not see very well, used his ears to hear the motion of the waves and the splash of the sea. He could hear the Kraken coming and shouted directions for the Captain to steer.

The pirate who couldn't hear set to work on the cannons. He could see very well, and his aim was perfect. He began firing on the Kraken with precision.

The large pirate who couldn't run very fast was very strong. He pulled on the sails to make the ship go faster as the wind filled the sails. His great strength kept them moving swiftly around the Kraken and away from danger.

The short pirate was so small he was able to move around the ship and avoid the Krakens arms. He dodged each arm, and used his size and speed to bring cannon balls to the crews cannons.

With all the water and seaweed coming over the rails of the ship the crew were slipping and sliding on the deck. Captain Jay, however, put his peg leg into one of the knots in his ship and kept his footing.

He stood there shouting orders and kept his crew calm, with Tiki holding tight to his shoulder.

All of his crew were doing great. Each pirate had their own special talent and, no matter how different they were, they all worked together as a team!

Suddenly the pirate with only one hand and a sharp hook in place of the other, ran to the front of the ship where the Kraken was starting charge. He waited, watching and measuring the distance until the exact moment the Kraken reached the ship.

Using his hook, the one-handed pirate cut the rope holding a giant net.

SWOOSH!

The net dropped and wrapped around the Kraken. The Kraken, caught in the net, released the other pirate Captains, their crews, and their ships. Captain Jay and his crew of misfits had saved the day!

The other Pirate Captains thanked Captain Jay, and apologized to him and his crew. They realized that just because a pirate is different does not mean they can't do things other pirates can. Each Captain offered Captain Jay's crew a spot on their ships, but each crew member declined!

The End.

CPSIA information can be obtained at www.ICGtesting.com
Printed in the USA
BVIW120945170319
542822BV00002B/4